To Joan,
with love,

Barclay

april 14, 1976

New Southern Poets

Selected Poems from *Southern Poetry Review*

Edited by
GUY OWEN and MARY C. WILLIAMS

The University of North Carolina Press
Chapel Hill

Copyright © 1974
The University of North Carolina Press
All rights reserved
Manufactured in the United States of America
ISBN 0-8078-1246-3
ISBN 0-8078-1240-4 (paper)
Library of Congress Catalog Card Number 74-19103

Library of Congress Cataloging in Publication Data

Owen, Guy, 1925-   comp.
  New Southern poets.

  1. American poetry—Southern States. I. Williams,
Mary C., 1923-   joint comp.   II. Southern poetry
review.   III. Title.
PS551.09   1975   811'.5'408   74-19103
ISBN 0-8078-1246-3
ISBN 0-8078-1240-4 (paper)

To Lodwick Hartley
and the former editors
of Southern Poetry Review

CONTENTS

ACKNOWLEDGMENTS

The editors are grateful to the following authors and publishers for permission to reprint poems from the works listed below:

Approaches for "Down Cellar," from *Down Cellar* by Prentice Baker. Copyright © 1972. Reprinted by permission of *Approaches*.

Atheneum for "The Temptress" and "The Metaphysician," from *Advantages of Dark* by Robert Watson. Copyright © 1966. Reprinted by permission of Atheneum.

The Basilisk Press for "The Cold Comes On," from *Mean Rufus Throw Down* by David J. Smith. Copyright © 1973 at Fredonia, New York. Reprinted by permission of The Basilisk Press.

George Braziller, Inc., for "Song," from *Welcome Eumenides* by Eleanor Ross Taylor; reprinted with the permission of the author and publisher. Copyright © 1972 by Eleanor Ross Taylor.

Drummer Press for "Down Zion's Alley," from *Down Zion's Alley* by Emily H. Wilson. Copyright © 1972. Reprinted by permission of Drummer Press.

Dryad Press for "Migrants," from *Something Tugging the Line* by Roderick Jellema. Reprinted by permission of Dryad Press.

Harcourt Brace Jovanovich, Inc., for "The Mad Farmer Revolution" and "A Praise," from *Farming: A Hand Book* by Wendell Berry. "The Mad Farmer Revolution" and "A Praise" are reprinted from *Farming: A Hand Book,* copyright © 1970 by Wendell Berry, by permission of Harcourt Brace Jovanovich, Inc.

Harper & Row for "Goat & Boy" and "The Mule," from *The Juice* by Coleman Barks, published by Harper & Row, copyright © 1972.

Alfred A. Knopf, Inc., for "Crazy Jane on Her Birthday," from *Adam's Dream* by Julia Randall. Copyright © 1969. Reprinted by permission of Alfred A. Knopf, Inc.

Moore Publishing Company for "The Dappled Ponies," from *Coming Out Even* by Campbell Reeves. Copyright © 1973. Reprinted by permission of Moore Publishing Company. "That Summer," from *To the Water's Edge* by Sam Ragan. Copyright © 1972. Reprinted by permission of Moore Publishing Company.

W. W. Norton & Company, Inc., for "Identity" and "Snow Log," from *Collected Poems* by A. R. Ammons. Copyright © 1972. Reprinted by permission of W. W. Norton & Co., Inc.

Olivant Press for "Down Here with Aphrodite," from *Devoirs to Florida* by

William E. Taylor. Copyright © 1968. Reprinted by permission of Olivant Press.

Rapp & Whiting for "The Legend of Paper Plates," from *The Stone Harp* by John Haines. Copyright © 1968. Reprinted by permission of Rapp & Whiting.

Red Clay Books for "The Policeman," from *East of Moonlight* by Julia Fields. Copyright © 1973. Reprinted by permission of Red Clay Books. "The Moon Is a Marrying Eye," from *The Moon Is a Marrying Eye* by Adrianne Marcus. Copyright © 1972. Reprinted by permission of Red Clay Books. "The Cremation of R. J.," from *Horse, Horse, Tyger, Tyger* by Heather Miller. Copyright © 1974. Reprinted by permission of Red Clay Books.

Rutgers University Press for "To a 14 Year Old Girl in Labor and Delivery" and "Resuscitation," from *The Smell of Matches* by John Stone. Copyright © 1972, Rutgers University, the State University of New Jersey. Reprinted by permission of Rutgers University Press.

South and West for "July Fourth Weather," from *Dust of the Sun* by Paul Baker Newman. Copyright © 1969. Reprinted by permission of South and West. "On Sundays We All Sat Around and Just Looked at One Another," from *Down Here With Aphrodite* by William E. Taylor. Copyright © 1966. Reprinted by permission of South and West.

Southern Poetry Review Press for "Epitaph Spoken by a Former Lover," "In an Ordinary Place," and "A Snowman in March," from *In an Ordinary Place* by Paul Ramsey. Copyright © 1965. Reprinted by permission of Southern Poetry Review Press.

Dabney Stuart for "The Warehouse Chute," from his book *The Diving Bell*. Copyright © 1966. Reprinted by permission of the author.

The University of Georgia Press for "A Question of Identity" by Catharine Savage Brosman, from *Watering* by Catharine Savage Brosman, copyright ©1972. Reprinted by permission of the University of Georgia Press.

University of Missouri Press for "For a Bitter Season," from *For a Bitter Season: New and Selected Poems* by George Garrett. Reprinted from *For a Bitter Season* by George Garrett, by permission of the author and the University of Missouri Press. Copyright © 1967 by George Garrett.

The University of North Carolina Press for "Another Ride with Goat McGuire," from *The Day I Stopped Dreaming about Barbara Steele* by R. H. W. Dillard. Copyright © 1966. Reprinted by permission of The University of North Carolina Press.

The University Press of Virginia for "Sleeping Out with My Father," from *A Program for Survival* by Gibbons Ruark. Copyright © 1971. Reprinted by permission of The University Press of Virginia.

Wesleyan University Press for "The Twin Falls," from *Drowning with Others* by James Dickey. Copyright © 1961 by James Dickey. Reprinted from

Drowning with Others, by James Dickey, by permission of Wesleyan University Press. "The Legend of Paper Plates," from *The Stone Harp* by John Haines. Copyright © 1968 by John Haines. Reprinted from *The Stone Harp*, by John Haines, by permission of Wesleyan University Press. "The News," from *Legion: Civic Choruses* by William Harmon. Copyright © 1973 by William Harmon. Reprinted from *Legion: Civic Choruses*, by William Harmon, by permission of Wesleyan University Press. "Caught in the Act," from *My Bones Being Wiser* by Vassar Miller. Copyright © 1962 by Vassar Miller. Reprinted from *My Bones Being Wiser*, by Vassar Miller, by permission of Wesleyan University Press. "The Tree Man at the Parthenon Tourist," from *Water Tables* by James Seay. Copyright © 1974 by James Seay. Reprinted from *Water Tables*, by James Seay, by permission of Wesleyan University Press.

The editors also wish to express their gratitude to the School of Liberal Arts, North Carolina State University, for a grant to aid in publication of this book.

INTRODUCTION

The publication of this anthology marks the fifteenth year of the existence of *Southern Poetry Review*. It was back in 1958 that Guy Owen, who was then teaching at Stetson University in Florida, became sufficiently disturbed about the absence of any local outlet for the publication of the creative work of his students that he decided to start a magazine of his own. With his own money he subsidized the printing of a publication he called *Impetus*, which was set into type and printed on an old hand press at Lake Como, Florida. Before very long *Impetus* was publishing not only student work but poetry by faculty and friends, until by the time Guy moved back to North Carolina to teach at North Carolina State University in Raleigh, he had a full-fledged poetry magazine on his hands. In 1964 *Impetus* became *Southern Poetry Review*, and became also what it remains today: a leading organ for the promulgation of poetry in the South, and one of the very best poetry magazines in the United States.

What I like most about *SPR* is the entire absence of cliquishness and coterie about its operation. What it does is to select the very best poetry it can get, from the best poets available, whether famous or unknown, and publish it in modest but attractive fashion. Just how high the quality of the magazine's poetry is can be seen in the fact that in 1973 no less than three of the poems in it were selected for the Borestone Mountain Awards for the best poems printed in the English language.

Why, it might be asked, do poetry magazines exist? There are so many of them, and so few survive beyond publication of a few issues. It has been my observation that most come into being to attain certain objectives, personal, political, and literary, of the editors. Many of our most important and influential poetry magazines have been of that sort. The more established magazines won't print poems that don't fulfill the editors' expectations of what poetry should be, and such expectations are based on the editors' own experience of poems that have been written and published in the past. When a poet or poets come along with something different, which doesn't fit these expectations, there is no place for such poems in the established magazines, so the only thing to do is for those who write and believe in the new poetry to establish magazines of their own. If they are right—which is to say, if they have something to say that is worth saying and that cannot be said in the established modes—then their magazine will find readers and the poems published in it will compel acceptance. When this objective is reached, the magazine is then no longer needed, for the more established magazines will have become receptive to the new way of imaging experience in words. If, on the other hand, the new kind of poetry doesn't "take," then the editors cash in their chips and try something else. In most instances it doesn't; there are always many poetic revolutionaries, but precious few poetic revolutions. The ultimate and inescapable test is pragmatic: does the new poetry being proffered have anything to say? If so, it will make its place. Poetry magazines are the vehicle by which the experiment is performed.

That is one kind of magazine, and a very necessary kind. *Southern Poetry Review*, however, is a different sort of poetry magazine. It doesn't have a Program; it is not the sounding board for ambitious young men with revolutions to achieve, axes to grind, and personal reputations to advance. The only objective of *SPR*, so far as I can tell, has been to publish good poetry, not merely by Southerners but from all over the world, and how well it has succeeded can be seen in this very impressive collection. Perhaps this way of going about things is one reason why, in not only surviving but flourishing for fifteen years, *SPR* has far eclipsed the national track record for most poetry magazines. Its editors love poetry, they will publish all the good poetry of any sort that they can find, and there are readers enough who rely upon their taste and judgment to keep the magazine going. Open the pages of the latest issue of *SPR* and you will find therein a supply of good poems by interesting poets; it is as simple—and editorially as difficult to do—as that.

For Guy Owen and his associates, in particular Max Halperen, Richard Goldsmith, Tom Walters, A. Sidney Knowles, and managing editor Mary C. Williams, bringing out *SPR* has been a labor of love. The time has passed, one is happy to say, when Guy and his associates were having to subsidize its publication with their own funds. Grants have been received from the North

Carolina Arts Council and the Coordinating Council for Little Magazines. Furthermore, *SPR* is even able to pay modest rates for its contributions, which is not only quite remarkable among poetry magazines but, the economics of the poetry world being what they are, insures it of being sent far more verse than it can possibly accommodate in its format. All in all, a success story, and Guy Owen, his magazine, and his university may take pride in it.

When one surveys the contents of this anthology, one realizes several things. One is that there are a number of very fine poets producing work today, and many of them are from the South. Another is that *SPR* has played an important role in encouraging and publishing a surprising number of very good poets early in their careers—as, for instance, A. R. Ammons, James Dickey, Fred Chappell, William E. Taylor, William Harmon, Wendell Berry, Van K. Brock, Robert Morgan, and Heather Miller, among others. And finally, one realizes just how much good can be done in the poetry world on very little money when a man really wants to do something and a university has the good sense to help him.

LOUIS D. RUBIN, JR.

New Southern Poets

BETTY ADCOCK

Things Left Standing

That summer I trailed the creek
every day daring to come
to the end of what I knew
with thin August water beside me,
the sun on the fields almost audible.

The last day, I turned with the creek
where a pine grove I had never seen
held a ruined country school
gutted, not by fire
but by hands of children
grown tall and permitted their will
of the unused.

In a coat of shadow and dead paint,
the walls seemed to fade, leaving outlines,
leaving one intact pane of glass
where the sun struck and gathered a shape
like the tow head of a child, one who was left
or whose ghost stayed unchanged
to study the seasons of corn.
Drawn in through a doorway of splinters,
I touched a broken desk, handled
the smell of wasps, housedust,
and pinewoods—the back wall was gone,
the room left open and legible.
Names were cut deep in three walls,
and shapes: every sexual part, all things
male and female were carved outsized,
were whole, new animals
in the wooden impossible book.

In the movement of shadow, that place
trembled with ritual, with the finding
that always is personless.
I spoke aloud to the fields

severed names, fragments, forbidden
words notched crookedly, correct.
I lay down near a tree,
slept, and my dream shaped a man
made simply of summer and grass,
who would take on a face, who would hold me
speaking the tongue of the touched.

When I woke to the noon beaten silence,
I stood up with the grass on my dress,
sharp stain that would stay.

The ghost that clouds any window
only at one angle of vision
was gone when I turned for home.

The thing that is given once,
or thrown like a curse or a weapon,
came both ways in the ruins of August.
I knew the dead child in the glass,
knew the sun with its open knife,
and I stood up without crying
from grass that smelled of the future
to wear as I must in time
the green deep scars of the light.

1974

Identity

1) an individual spider web
identifies a species:

an order of instinct prevails
through all accidents of circumstance,

though possibility is
high along the peripheries of
spider
webs:
you can go all
around the fringing attachments

and find
disorder ripe,
entropy rich, high levels of random,
numerous occasions of accident

2) the possible settings
of a web are infinite:

how does
the spider keep
identity
while creating the web
in a particular place?

how and to what extent
and by what modes of chemistry
and control?

it is
wonderful
how things work: I will tell you
about it
because

it is interesting
and because whatever is
moves in weeds
   and blood and spider webs
and known
               is loved
      and in that love,
      each of us knowing it,
      I love you,

for how it moves beyond us,
          sizzles in
winter grasses, darts and hangs with bumblebees
by summer windowsills!

              I will show you
the underlying that takes no image of itself
but weaves in and out of moons and bladderweeds
            and is all and
      beyond destruction
      because created fully in no
particular form:

              if the web were perfectly pre-set,
              the spider would
      never find
      a perfect place to set in it: and
           if the web were

perfectly adaptable,
if freedom and possibility were without limit,
          the web would
lose its special identity:

      the row-strung garden web
keeps order at the center
where space is freest (interesting that the freest
      "medium" should
      accept the firmest order)

and that
order
                    diminishes toward the
periphery
            allowing at the points of contact
                        entropy equal to entropy:

1963

Snow Log

Especially the fallen tree
the snow picks
out in the woods to show:

the snow means nothing by that
no special emphasis: actually
snow picks nothing out:

but was it a failure, is it,
snow's responsible for
that the brittle upright black

shrubs and small trees
set off what caught the snow
in special light:

or there's some intention
behind the snow snow's too shallow
to reckon with: I take it on myself:

especially the fallen tree
the snow picks
out in the woods to show.

1970

JAMES APPLEWHITE

A Vigil

I.

Thanksgiving sacrament, piety of crystal and silver.
Platters and dishes passed on from hand to hand.
Words so well-worn they drone with the summertime fan.
My grandfather blessing, his countenance fields in the sunlight.

I waited beside him for words, for what he'd gathered
From hawks wheeling sun, oak leaves' tension under glare.
He rocked in the parlor with a bible, his face grown taciturn,
The hooked nose indian, hair as if filamented down.
His parchment skin was the season's hieroglyphic.
Going for water, I passed through the company parlor:
Mantel with mirror and clock, stiff plush and varnish.

II.

One window overlooked the trees of the creek, where silt
From high water on leaves seemed dust from days passing by.

I poured from a pitcher. Tracing a beaded trickle,
Sweat down a frosted tumbler. Sensation of October
In August. I thirsted to bring into potable solution
These motes of dust that swam the green shade's sunbeam.
I sat on the porch beside him, spell-bound by columns.
Horizon woven to softening by orbits of swallows.

"It's been eighty-six years and it seems like a day."

1974

Down Cellar

Harshly the wind all day has tossed the hedges
And threshed the yellow trees up the stone stair.
There are four citrons here, sitting on ledges,
And three white kraut crocks and a broken chair.
Dust motes, borne down diagonal shafts of light,
Escape the delicious tumult of this weather.
I sit here on the last step, out of sight,
Sheltered and warm and withdrawn altogether.
Seen through the slant rectangle of the door,
The sky stands blue and bottomless, upside down.
Inquisitive of what I sit here for,
A buff hen and a white hen and a brown
Look fussily down as if to say, "Come out;
Down cellar, where the golden motes descend,
and in the gloomy company of kraut
And citrons, you will never taste the wind."
Shadowless on the treetops lashed and bending
Cold sunlight streams and leaves are torn away.
Flailing the hedges there has blown unending
Out of the sky: the wind harshly all day.

1972

COLEMAN BARKS

The Mule

get up under a mule
sometime and look   you

may have heard wrong:
the equipment's all there

dormant   dreaming
of some great mythical

union between species
like Leda & her Swan

or the God-Bull & Europa:
the mule is an aristocrat, one

of the last Classical allusions
in this illiterate world

1971

Goat & Boy

rocking motion of remembering: red pig-iron gate latch
now my feet are on the tree roots   just inside the fence
hyaah   hyaaah   to scare him away   like I've seen done
this goat with eyes broken red inside   his head even
with mine   the horns glance off my shoulder into ivy
the screen door that I run to   is locked from inside
a hoof on the step behind me   then his goatface dressed
in a strand of ivy   waiting for me to take hold of
years ridged into horn   conch shell in my hands
slowly rocking side to side   neither of us with arms
deadlocked in a zodiac of child & goat   a period piece
without a sound or a cry   but moving on its own

1969

GERALD W. BARRAX

Moby Christ

Again, Father,
I've tried to escape the tyranny of your right hand—
how many times among those fools who never know me
until it's too late
and now as lord of these hosts of the waters.

Again, Father,
you've searched me out—
once Judas
and now the divine madness of an old man
to hound me down to the sea like an animal.

My scars multiply:
you'll fill my skin with harpoons
as you've filled my memory with your crosses—
what I must pay
to put spirit into flesh,
to feel, God, to feel
even the pain.
You are old, Father,
a fond and foolish old man
who has never known that much
about what you've created.

        My hosts will pay, too.
Men believe I once died for their sins
and now these great creatures will die for mine:
        there go the ships, Father,
on your wide sea which your wanton boys
will wash in Leviathan's blood
and hunt down to extinction.

When the sea gives up its dead
Father
will nothing rise from its depths
but the fools who have crawled over the earth?

1972

SCOTT BATES

Guide to the Eiffel Tower

From the top of this phallus
You can see to the palace
Which
With the blessing of Jesus
And plenty of class
King Louis Quatorze and his
Whores built for picnics
Out of nothing but peasants
And pieces of glass

1968

The Ballad of
Thoughtful Love

Of a nun they tell in a chilly cell
In medieval weather
Who loved her lady Mary well
But loved her freedom better

When Spring was at its handsomest
Went winging like a swallow
To find a fair and warmer nest
In a busy town bordello

Wherein she lived for many years
Of fleshly fascinations

[13]

Till certain little demon fears
Of deep incinerations

Restored her to her chilly cell
—Where nobody had missed her
Sweet Mary having played so well
Her role as faithful sister

—Which proves I guess a moral of
Sin-sacrifice-salvation
As well as one of thoughtful love
That saves much explanation

1971

Kilroy Turtle

The nurse in the rainbow
Dress dances like her breasts
Are as untouched as the palm
Of the world's newest surgical glove.

Were I Dr. Kilroy instead
Of just Kilroy, S.O.B.,
I'd be very important and snug
Her as closely as water
Hugs rock apples,

My rubbery fingers
Fumbling ten soft roots
For a grip on the world,

My tongue ready to leap,
A trout,
Out of my mouth
Into the very whorl itself;

Instead, I'm Kilroy Turtle
And don't come out and that
Quickly her smile is gone
As she walks by and smiles.

1973

WENDELL BERRY

The Mad Farmer Revolution,
Being a Fragment
Of the Natural History of New Eden,
In Homage to Mr. Ed McClanahan,
One of the Locals

The mad farmer, the thirsty one,
went dry. When he had time
he threw a visionary high
lonesome on the holy communion wine.
"It is an awesome event
when an earthen man has drunk
his fill of the blood of a god,"
people said, and got out of his way.
He plowed the churchyard, the
minister's wife, three graveyards
and a golf course. In a parking lot
he planted a forest of little pines.
He sanctified the groves,
dancing at night in the oak shades
with goddesses. He led
a field of corn to creep up
and tassel like an Indian tribe
on the court house lawn. Pumpkins
ran out to the ends of their vines
to follow him. Ripe plums
and peaches reached into his pockets.
Flowers sprang up in his tracks
everywhere he stepped. And then
his planter's eye fell on
that parson's fair fine lady
again. "O holy plowman," cried she,
"I am all grown up in weeds.
Pray, bring me back into good tilth."
He tilled her carefully

and laid her by, and she
did bring forth others of her kind,
and others, and some more.
They sowed and reaped till all
the countryside was filled
with farmers and their brides sowing
and reaping. When they died
they became two spirits of the woods.
On their graves were written
these words without sound:
"Here lies Saint Plowman.
Here lies Saint Fertile Ground."

1969

A Praise

His memories lived in the place
like fingers locked in the rock ledges
like roots. When he died
and his influence entered the air
I said, Let my mind be the earth
of his thought, let his kindness
go ahead of me. Though I do not escape
the history barbed in my flesh,
certain wise movements of his hands,
the turns of his speech
keep with me. His hope of peace
keeps with me in harsh days,
the shell of his breath dimming away
three summers in the earth.

1968

DORIS BETTS

The Marrying Woman

What lies between my legs is feast
as well as hungry beast; I'm such
an aged modern,
younger than mama but not much
and not enraged.
I want his touch upon my pubic hair,
not mine, not hers.
Giving is got
and unfair time
swallows us (one lump
or two?)
Circle my finger gold before
it bends; enfold
this folding face, these breasts
that will slope however kissed.
I hope to have his same hands
catch those sliding cells.
I need to know my tongue is home
in two mouths, and to bleed
my moons serenely, breed sons who own
his brown eye and my blue.
I want to die two times—
the little and big deaths—
in the same bed with him,
with you! With you.

Hard is the skull in my soft head.
I want my coming bones
to be comforted.

1973

VAN K. BROCK

Peter's Complaint

I

After supper, we argued over stars
While you went off, saying, "Keep watch for soldiers."
But supper was too heavy and we slept.

You woke us with such quiet admonishment
That, seeing the flares, I was whelmed with guilt
And would have killed a fellow with my knife
Had you not stopped me, saying, "I'll go," and gone
To show us what your words had always meant.

But seeing word as fact, I felt betrayed
And said, "I never knew him in my life."

II

Hidden in my mantle, in the mob,
Planning to purge my flesh of a sick dream,
I watched you hung, outstretched, above our heads.

The sun grew black in eclipse, ringed thin with light,
Then was itself again, so suddenly
That those who watched grew blind. Terror had turned
My dark eyes inward. It was then you died.

III

Since we had met in groves often at night,
I found it harder now to reconcile
Your sunburned flesh, your new, translucent face.

Yet having to wear a beard taught compromise:
I! Me! a native of the oath.
Egyptian, Persian, Greek and Roman—we

Saw all powers turning on one spit,
The light and dark, flesh, mind and spirit.

They hung me upside down. The nails were keys
To kingdoms—the empire, then its conquerors.

IV

Authority had so fixed our eyes on quiet
Atriums that we, inured to nature now,
Judged all landscapes by our secluded gardens.
Triumphant, we became the absolute,
Bent men to God, burned books, castrated statues,
Structured time, foreshadowed revolutions.

Cathedrals of stressed logic, bound and buttressed
By new hierarchic heraldry, told our story.
The Word, woven into stone-dark facades
That anchored tall shafts spanned with colored glass,
Held up our stone tents, pitched high in the air.

Spirit infused matter, *mater omnium,*
Chanted new quantums, through stained and filtered dark,
While under drowsing lids we worshipped light.

V

Mist in a wind, the light of ancience, distilled,
Began to rain and freshen stagnant water.
When everything withers into the new year,
While winter holds time frozen in its mind,
We do not know what new thoughts spring will have.

The stars have grown too great to comprehend,
Too far (or near) to argue, and turned from silver
To flame. The blood runs upward toward the brain.
Our minds grow younger while our hearts grow old.

But God inhabits, while eluding, all ideas
And will be found again in wind and waves,
Subject, like us, to fortune and to rumor.

The churches crowd the planet of hunger. Children
Make crosses of sticks and wish for food—
Awed at your monuments, museums of torture
Devices: the cross itself, edicts against
Prevention and abortion, the anomalies of birth,
Pickled grotesqueries.

Crosses orbit. Cathedrals spin toward the moon.

VI

I try to remember if you are what we remembered,
But cannot clearly remember you—
And never saw you clearly. When we both were,
The air was always filled with vapors of dawn,
The dust of day, the haze of twilight, starlight.
Our sight was never steady or finely shaded.
And I was not a rock. It surprises me
They say you said so. What I was is vague
Even to me. For I have been confused
With fact and legend since that old impermanence.
Even as I speak I am being altered.

VII

Though we have been hard grains in the sieve,
We dissolve in streams, disperse, and strained by earth,
Are assumed again by time, crossed with dream.
On the rack constellations of the night,
The motion of the wheel grinds and scatters in space
Until we rain out of abyss itself.

But the heart's savage mob forcing our door
Is crying for blood, the old sacrament,
Though we have turned, like all magic, to myth.
Thus they are turning from us and we from them.
Yet we are shackled, ourselves a cross, to stars
That twist us as they turn and turn and turn.

1971

Lying on a Bridge

We saw anchored worlds in a shallow stream.
The current tugged at clouds, the sun, our faces.
And while we stared, as though into a dream,
The stream moved on; the anchors kept their places.
Even the white rose thorned into your hair
Stayed there, though its refracted, scattered aura
Circled your abstract face, like snow in air;
Then the rose fell onto that gentle water,
Shattering our faces with their mirror. But sun
And clouds, and all their height and depth of light,
Could not feel so involved, nor watch when one
Bloom touched that current and waltzed it out of sight.
Though rising, we saw how all things float in space:
The stars and clouds, ourselves, each other's face.

1967

CATHARINE SAVAGE BROSMAN

A Question of Identity

See how the shore receded in the dark
as the tide rose: tracks of crabs
which we came to read, moon-pulled, at midnight

become cuneiform on the sea floor;
waves wash the flank of the road
and patches of grass are swallowed in the sway,

sway of water, the bubbly wreaths
visited on the drowned. Boundaries seem too
uncertain: overnight the line can change

between the loose, terrible sea
which can pull my legs out in the undertow
and the sands where I have taken hold.

My dreams of drowning revive: I can already
feel the breakers beating at my bones; old
live oaks may succumb at last to liquid.

Are all our questions still to be re-asked?
perhaps the very dryness of the land,
the wetness of the wet called into doubt?

But wait: the tide turns, and the zenith sun
sheds demarcation on the shore,
and the changing wind says   that this

is the truth of the bay:
all things must have an edge, keeping
identity, however tenuous; even space

that crashes into gaseous ruffs of stars;
oceans exhausting themselves
in shallow inlets; even a storm which is turned

back, as the trees resist. And that the ends
of things, stream, continent, or a love
splintering against a sandbar

—all peripheries—are, in their dual light,
also the center of reality—since
we know the world by differences,

the sea by the way it floods a shelf of beach,
and the wind, by its dervish shape
among antennaed dunes.

1967

The New Dolores Leather Bar

> I adjure thee, respond from thine altars,
>   Our Lady of Pain.
>   —A. C. Swinburne

Not quite alone from night to night you'll find them.
Who need so many shackles to remind them
Must doubt that they are prisoners of love.

The leather creaks; studs shine: the chain mail jingles.
Shoulders act as other forms of bangles
In a taste where push has come to shove.

So far from hardhats and so near to Ziegfeld,
They, their costume, fail.   Trees felled, each twig felled,
One sees the forest: Redneck Riding Hood's.

Does better-dear-to-eat-you drag, with basket,
Make the question moot?   Go on and ask it.
Red, do you deliver, warm, the goods?

Or is the axle-grease, so butch an aura,
Underneath your nails in fact mascara?
Caution, lest your lie, your skin unscarred,

Profane these clanking precincts of the pain queen.
Numb with youth, an amateur procaine queen,
In the rite you lose the passage.   Hard,

To know the hurt the knowledge.   Command is late now,
Any offer master of your fate now.
You can, though won't, escape.   Tarnishing whore,

So cheap your metal and so thin your armor,
Fifteen years will have you once more farmer.
Mammon values; earth and pain ignore.
Name your price and serve him well before.

1974

FRED CHAPPELL

My Grandmother Washes Her Feet

I see her still, unsteadily riding the edge
Of the clawfoot tub, mumbling to her feet,
Musing bloodrust water about her ankles.
Cotton skirt pulled up, displaying bony
Bruised patchy calves that would make you weep.

Rinds of her soles had darkened, crust-colored—
Not yellow now—like the tough outer belly
Of an adder. In fourteen hours the most refreshment
She'd given herself was dabbling her feet in the water.

"You mightn't've liked John-Giles, Everybody knew
He was a mean one, galloping whiskey and bad women
All night. Tried to testify dead drunk
In church one time. *That* was a ruckus. Later
Came back a War Hero, and all the young men
Took to doing the things he did. And failed.
Finally one of his women's men shot him."

"What for?"

                    "Stealing milk through fences . . . That part
Of Family nobody wants to speak of.
They'd rather talk about fine men, brick houses,
Money. Maybe you ought to know, teach you
Something."

          "What *do* they talk about?"

                              "Generals,
And the damn Civil War, and marriages.
Things you brag about in the front of Bibles.
You'd think there was arms and legs of Family
On every battlefield from Chickamauga
To Atlanta."

          "That's not the way it is?"

"Don't matter how it is. No proper way
To talk, is all. It was nothing they ever did.
And plenty they *won't* talk about . . . John-Giles!"

Her cracked toes thumped the tub wall, spreading
Shocklets. Amber toenails curled like shavings.
She twisted the worn knob to pour in coolness
I felt suffuse her body like a whiskey.

"Bubba Martin, he was another, and no
Kind of man. Jackleg preacher with the brains
Of a toad. Read the Bible upsidedown and crazy
Till it drove him crazy, making crazy marks
On doorsills, windows, sides of Luther's barn.
He killed hisself at last with a shotgun.
No gratitude for Luther putting him up
All those years. Shot so he'd fall down the well."

"I never heard."

                    "They never mention him.
Nor Aunt Annie, that everybody called
Paregoric Annie, that roamed the highways
Thumbing cars and begging change to keep
Even with her craving. She claimed she was saving up
To buy a glass eye. It finally shamed them
Enough, they went together and got her one.
That didn't stop her. She lugged it around
In a velvet-lined case, asking strangers
Please to drop it in the socket for her.
They had her put away. And that was that.
There's places Family ties just won't stretch to."

Born then in my mind a race of beings
Unknown and monstrous. I named them Shadow-Cousins,
A linked long dark line of them,
Peering from mirrors and gleaming in closets, agog
To manifest themselves inside myself.
Like discovering a father's cancer.
I wanted to search my body for telltale streaks.

"Sounds like a bunch of cow thieves."

"Those too, I reckon,
But they're forgotten or covered over so well
Not even I can make them out. Gets foggy
When folks decide they're coming on respectable.
First thing you know, you'll have a Family Tree."

(I imagined a wind-stunted horse-apple.)

She raised her face. The moons of the naked bulb
Flared in her spectacles, painting out her eyes.
In dirty water light bobbed like round soap.
A countenance matter-of-fact, age-engraven,
Mulling in peaceful wonder petty annals
Of embarrassment. Gray but edged with brown
Like an old photograph, her hair shone yellow.
A tiredness mantled her fine energy.
She shifted, sluicing water under instep.

"O what's the use," she said. "Water seeks
Its level. If your daddy thinks that teaching school
In a white shirt makes him a likelier man,
What's to blame. Leastways, he won't smother
Of mule-farts or have to starve for a pinch of rainfall.
Nothing new gets started without the old's
Plowed under, or halfway under. We sprouted from dirt,
Though, and it's with you, and dirt you'll never forget."

"No Mam."

                "Don't you say me No Mam yet.
Wait till you get your chance to deny it."

Once she giggled, a sound like stroking muslin.

"You're bookish. I can see you easy a lawyer
Or a county clerk in a big white suit and tie,
Feeding the preacher and bribing the sheriff and the judge.
Second-generation-respectable
Don't come to any better destiny.
But it's dirt you rose from, dirt you'll bury in.
Just about the time you'll think your blood

Is clean, here will come dirt in a natural shape
You never dreamed. It'll rise up saying, Fred,
Where's that mule you're supposed to march behind?
Where's your overalls and roll-your-owns?
Where's your Blue Tick hounds and Domineckers?
Not all the money in this world can wash true-poor
True rich. Fatback just won't change to artichokes."

"What's artichokes?"

                    "Pray Jesus you'll never know.
For if you do it'll be a sign you've grown
Away from what you are, can fly to pieces
Like a touch-me-not . . . I may have errored
When I said *true-poor.* It ain't the same
As dirt-poor. When you got true dirt you got
Evérything you need . . . and don't you say me
Yes Mam again. You just wait."

                   She leaned
And pulled the plug. The water circled gagging
To a bloody eye and poured in the hole like a rat.
I thought maybe their spirits had gathered there,
All my Shadow-Cousins clouding the water,
And now they ran to earth and would cloud the earth.
Effigies of soil, I could seek them out
By clasping soil, forcing warm rude fingers
Into ancestral jelly my father wouldn't plow.
I strained to follow them, and never did.
I never had the grit to stir those guts.
I never had the guts to stir that earth.

1973

The Twin Falls

Upon the light, bare, breathless water
To step, and thereby be given a skiff
That hangs by its nose to the bank
And trembles backward:

To stand on those boards like a prince
Whose kingdom is still as a cloud,
And through it, like a road through Heaven,
The river moves:

To sink to the floor of the boat
As into a deep, straining coffin,
And in one motion come from my mother,
Loose the long cord:

To lie here timelessly flowing
In a bed that lives like a serpent,
And thus to extend my four limbs
From the spring to the sea:

To look purely into the sky,
As the current possesses my body
Like a wind, and blows me through
Land I have walked on,

And all in a pattern laid down
By rain, and the forces of age,
Through banks of red clay, and cane-fields,
And the heart of a forest:

And at dusk to hear the far falls
Risingly roaring to meet me,
And, set in that sound, eternal
Excitement of falling:

And yet, strangely, still to be
Upheld on the road to Heaven
Through the changing, never-changed earth
Of this lived land:

And now in all ways to be drunken,
With a mind that can lift up my body
In all the grounded music of the dead
Now nearer their rising:

To do nothing but rest in my smile,
With nothing to do but go downward
Simply when water shall fall
In the mineral glimmer

Of the lightning that lies at the end
Of the wandering path of escape
Through the fields and green clouds of my birth,
And bears me on,

Ecstatic, indifferent, and
My mother's son, to where insupportable water
Shall dress me in blinding clothes
For my descent.

1959

R. H. W. DILLARD

Another Ride with Goat McGuire

for Louis D. Rubin, Jr.

Old Goat McGuire, his whisky breath,
Remembers, lifts his head to laugh,
Two crummies and a load of dynamite,
The snow that night, the northern pines
All black and white, the burning wood,
Steam up, the bell, the engine and
Those turning wheels, snow blew, and Goat,
Old Goat McGuire came through.

Long ago that ride. Too long now.
No cars rattle on that logging track,
The woods all stumped and gullied out,
And Goat more wrinkled than he was before.
The barn door bangs, car barn, round
House, the engines gone, not even rust
Remains.

        Perhaps a handcar sits hidden
In the dust, dark in a shadow, no corner
For the house is round; but then no car,
No wheels at all, and Goat, old Goat,
His whisky breath, looks all around
And leaves.

        No work here and now,
His bottle empty (it clatters and then
Shatters in the cluttered tracks,
In the dry and weedy dark), Goat
Turns onto the open road, weaves down
The track, no red light (or green),
No arms salute his smoking breath,
The track is clear.

And back in town
The diesels pass, the long cars tiered
With automobiles, the boxcars and the angry
Horns. No, that's no world for Goat
McGuire, hero of a snowy night, two
Crummies and a load of dynamite. Old
Goat, he wanders down the track, turns
Off and down the bank, heads home, his
Whisky breath, his sagging bed, so warm,
His old and sleeping wife. Street lights
Glow green, three trees that hold their leaves
And keep them green despite the night,
The coming cold. He whistles, long and low,
Claps down his arms, and Goat, Old Goat McGuire
Goes home.

1966

GERALD DUFF

Here Where I Am Able to Wake

Always in that dream
the woman who was my wife
is not at home, late again

It is night, quiet, I am living
in the North woods
the snow is deep, the air cold and cracked

At three in the night of the dream
she comes with small noises
on a tall horse, black and wide

Her dress is uniform

She sits erect and silent
I come to the door of the cabin,
the moon full against the cold

and ask her to come in

She refuses
speaks in general terms
of my general failure
promises never to see me again
and rides slowly across the clearing
into the dark woods

I go back to bed in the cabin
and find myself easily asleep . . .
twice unconscious

there in the dream in the cabin
and here where I am able to wake . . .

1973

The Model

She stood with her back to him like a white vase
Ready to receive whatever emotion
He might pour into her—At first, just this,
She the receiver, he the virile pitcher.
They must start as objects or not at all:
The curve of her hip felt at a distance,
The alabaster handles of her arms.
It was the liquid that would unite them,
The man carved like a troll, satyr, god.
Having placed her, as he began to paint,
Her silence would cry out, "Locate me!"
Then she would turn, mouth open like the lip
Of a vase, toward the tilted, brimming man
And a whole wash of colors would pour out
The red, yellow, blue, the lilac Venus—
So much has been said about this transfer,
The rich, brusque techniques, juxtapositions,
The man now empty and the woman full,
Her porcelain breasts alive as rosebuds,
But too little of how a man may live
Somewhat at peace without his poured emotions—
The girl walks the street now, vital forever,
Equipped with much more than she needs for love,
As though another sympathy had just
Been added to whatever contains us all.

1970

JULIA FIELDS

The Policeman

The policeman
            leaves his beat
            follows me,
                        an iron abstract
                        of phallus
                                    dangling
                                                from
                                                        his
                                                                hips.

                        He leans
                        with the studied disinterest—
                        the cold casualness of spies
                        thieves dogs and traitors
                                    against
                                    a tree
                                                of newspapers.

            My movement is his noose. I, a thief who filches sun and
                                    air and rain
                                    and the toasting
                                    warm aroma of
                                    cashews and buns.

            In my sweet solitude in the streets in the midst of crowds
            I baffle the
                        checkerboard mind
                                                of
                                                        the
                                                                blue
                                                                        man;

The checkerboard
                mind
                blocks the
                        traffic
                                of
                                    the
                                        world.

I walk him round
                n
                round
                    n
                    round.

1973

GEORGE GARRETT

For a Bitter Season

The oak tree in my front yard dies,
whose leaves are sadder than cheap wrapping paper,
and nothing I can do will keep it long.

Last spring in another place my pear tree
glistened in bloom like a graceful drift of snow.
Birds and bees loved that spacious white,

and a daughter was born in the time of flowers.

Now I am a stranger and my oak tree dies
young. Blight without a name, a bad omen.
I, too, die daily, fret in my familiar flesh,

and I take this for a bitter season.
We have lived too long with fear. We take
fear for granted like a drunken uncle,

like a cousin not quite all there
who's always there. I have lived too long
with the stranger who haunts my mirror.

Night in the city and the siren screams
fresh disasters for my morning paper.
The oak tree in the front yard dies.

Bless us, a houseful of loving strangers,
one good woman, two small boys, a man
waking from silence to cough his name.

Bless my daughter made of snow and bluest eyes.

1962

The Death of Martin Collins

Martin, when you died, I remembered you
at slaughtering: how you eased
the hog down the mouth of the oil drum
into the scalding water, and scraped
the hide, your knife blade shivering
down the skin; how you hung him
by his hamstrings from a tree and split
the tension of the flesh to let
the entrails spill in a shattering fall
of blood over the brim of your hands.

And I remembered dreaming of you
riding in that carcass, huddled
dying in the hog's boned hull,
floating like moonlight on a lake,
a shoreless hero adrift.

You have left me only death.
And I cling to it as if it were my own.

1970

JOHN HAINES

The Legend of Paper Plates

They trace their ancestry
back to the forest.
There all the family stood,
proud, bushy, and strong.

Until hard times,
when from fire and drought
the patriarchs crashed.

The land was taken for taxes,
the young people cut down
and sold to the mills.

Their manhood and womanhood
was crushed, bleached
with bitter acids,
their fibres dispersed
as sawdust
among ten million offspring.

You see these at any picnic,
at ballgames, at home,
and at state occasions.

They are thin and pliable,
porous and identical.
They are made to be thrown away.

1969

O. B. HARDISON

Speculation

Across the void's indifferent flood
The atoms drift like subtle snow;
In metaphysical cold blood
They'll kill the mind that thought them so.

Not warmth or light or subtle I
That's crucified on its own stick,
Or soundness or infirmity
Exist within the Ding an sich.

Outside titanic powers rave
and batter at our puny walls;
Let us be thankful for our cave
And whistle till the ceiling falls.

Yet I would gladly leave this home
And naked in some flowering south
Extract like honey from the comb
The gold essential of your mouth.

1961

Girl with Guitar

To S. G.

See on those six high wires how her fingers
In a flickering dance (though random to my dazzled
Eye) defy the deep, and balancing on touch
Imponderable, measure the trembling lines,

Gamut from grumbling bass to glittering treble,
And strike the note of peril that we live.

And now involved in moving harmonies
Whose motions are the nations of the air
Whose time is pattern shifting in the light,
The heart grown reckless from those airs of grace
And tunes of glory, vibrates on its pegs,
And she, all glitter in the golden fields,
Alone and splendid, is its only song.

1964

WILLIAM HARMON
The News

the latest from South Dakota.

the boy in blue pulled up a parking meter & used it to beat a buffalo to
   death this morning on the main street of Sioux Falls.
where in the name of heaven did the great beast come from.
what was he doing on the wrong side of the street the avalanche of
   untidy upholstery the unspeakable liquid mixtures dripping from
   his black ripped lips.
& could that yawing cue actually have been a penis.

the verso of the nickel now shows Monticello a structure humped some-
   what like a buffalo.
but hardly the kind of entity to go tearing unshod mind you unshod down
   the chartered pavement of Sioux Falls.
Monticello keeps its broad mouth shut.
like someone who has given birth to a fire & knows how it burns.

so merciful heaven.
thank you for cops whose winged shields have not yet deprived them of
   the blessed presence of mind to grab the nearest bludgeon cudgel
   or even parking meter with twelve minutes left on it & brain that.
that unmannered beast.
because who knows one may now & again see fit to rampage down the
   main street of Sioux Falls or someplace else why who can say.
mercy me.

it took place happened between the morning rush & the lunch hour the
   slack time when policemen ordinarily relax.
so Sioux Falls can count itself lucky that one man was alert for other-
   wise that.
unprepossessing buffalo would have turned china shops literally.
scenes of unexampled carnage friends & neighbors blasted plate glass
   into supernovae butterflies underinsured maidenheads God-
   jammed radio stations haywire.
anvils dropped into dishpans & turds in cut-glass punchbowls amok.
berserk undignified foreign-looking plus on top of it all a shifting hump
   of saturated fat & gristle.

1972

EUGENE HOLLAHAN

Stone Mountain: the True Moment

If a bird cast itself across the stone's face
Altering the impersonal proud rock so it changed
To the bland backdrop of a significant act.

If the bird spoke to you across the water
(Which moved too, as the bird moved, with the wind's caress
Both moving with the slow gestures of the living trees).

If you saw the bird throw itself athwart the bleak grey rock
(Where you lay on the sand under the flaming sun).
If you cast your heart upon the water in a gesture of response.

If you turned from your pleasure or pain, forgetting your self,
And watched the bird juxtaposed upon the stone like a wish in a
       dream,
Not from an eye's corner but exclusive and direct.

That bird is still flying against the rock's paralyzed face
The water and trees and air are your companions still
The pain and pleasure you abjured are what, at this or any moment,
       you will be.

1973

JOSEPHINE JACOBSEN

The Rock-Plant Wife

The rock-plant wife is dead.
She failed to overwinter.
Along with the rare peony and most
of the candy-tuft
she is gone.

A cell bloomed in her body
one icy night, hoped in her warmth;
was not disappointed;
sent its seed along her flesh,
its garden; like clover
took over that small space.

Now she herself is planted like a bulb.
Three of my friends are down there since first snow,
in that great soil where roots and rocks
and friends turn
with my turning world
but do not turn to me.

The rock-plant husband moves among the rocks.
He could not keep his wife or peony.
He says her name;
and sends his spade into a shallow hump
for my dwarf-iris clump,
while friends of mine turn
silently in deeper soil.
I touched them, and they, me. We had
kisses and arguments and silences, all different.
Now I have the last.

The clump is up,
blue as our summer day.
He, like any gardener,
believes in spring. Today
(*pace* the gardener) in summer
spring is too far.

1973

[45]

Breaking and Entering

She turns from the priest
potent and humble:
between her teeth
God breaks and crumbles.

Fair enough. God eats her slowly:
senses, friends, powers;
attitudes, energy;
ah, hours.

She eats Him quickly, neat.
This is her body and He in it;
what here she eats
breeds a live minute

to set against days
catatonic, demented.
Also, to rescue her
another love has entered

humanly. Entries have sown green
where ice held the fort.
She has broken love; been entered, seen
green in the desert.

She counts her life by such
breaking and entering:
understanding touch
as central to God, man, woman.

1974

Migrants

Birds obeying migration maps etched in their brains
Never revised their Interstate routes.
Some of them still stop off in Washington, D.C.

This autumn evening as the lights of the Pentagon
Come on like the glare of urgent trouble through surgery skylights,
Come on like a far-off hope of control,

I watch a peaceful V-sign of Canada Geese
Lower their landing gear, slip to rest on the slicky Potomac,
Break rank and huddle with the bobbing power boats.

Wings of jets are beating the air, taking turns for the landing—
Pterodactyls circling the filled-in swamps under National Airport.
There is a great wild honking

Of traffic on the bridges—
The daily homing of migrants with headlights dimmed
Who loop and bank by instinct along broken white lines.

1970

DONALD JUSTICE

To My Poems

on their being left out of
an anthology entitled THE
NEW AMERICAN POETRY

Now you pay for every crime
You were driven to by rhyme,
Rhyme and reason and the rest.
It is folly to protest.
With your craft, with your art
You were guilty from the start.
Were you not begotten in
Meter, our great parents' sin,
First, original, and worst?
For that alone you were accurst.

1962

DAVID MADDEN

Leda and the Paratrooper

Wind Marched along the line,
Pins clenched on slip and hose
She saw. Lux crisping
On her soap-suds wrists,
She ran across grass tender
As hymen against horn, toward
Blowing silk and eye-white birches.
Fingers reaching among rippling silk,
She watched a speck on the sun
Become a parachute, become a bird,
Become a parachute, and, poised
On her toes, watched it come down,
Wind-stiff, as silk stung her cheek.
Flying over cloven field,
She saw him land and stagger,
The chute drag him on his back;
She, apron slung, house dress
From throat to knee undone
Flung herself upon him
Where he rocked on a ruffle of silk,
Clouds still turning in his belly,
Sun on the tip of his tongue,
Still the sky turning in the expiring silk.

1966

ADRIANNE MARCUS

The Moon Is a Marrying Eye

Suspicion swells my breasts each month;
At 35 the nipples darken with the moon.
The dumb scars quiver on my belly
Where my children burned like rainbows.

And when it comes, red and terrifying,
This is the secret my legs hide: Female
And sister, what rides in my blood
Owes me five days a month.

Where is my child? Empty and loose,
My body is bearing itself away.
Who will demand my white empty arms,
My ancestral armor, my bones?

1971

The Cremation of R.J.

We are not to think of Christ Church
where the poet,
dead on his bier,
lay catnapping nine lives.

Upstairs on Fisher Park Circle,
we girls combed out our long bright tortoise locks,
snapping electricity,
curling
purring to the lascivious comb.

Cheshire seasons dazzle me now,
so many cremations later,
the sunny-striped grass,
sycamores like orange explosion,
crisp,
cured,
tied off to stand in a shock and dry.

The Halloween candles return me to my flesh,
giving its light straight-out naked,
in a raw rind,
grinning—
    melted in the morning
    down to a
      formless
        babe.

I keep hearing the match rasp against my bones,
my hair goes up in a yellow corona,

and these eyes flare out.
I eclipse the moon,
each fingernail a fiery spear.

Cheshire,
see me grin back.
Wake up and start, nine lives.

1972

In a Difficult Time

everything that was true becomes a lie.
There was no spring that murmured in my dreams,
no quarter-moon riding it like a bright
canoe, no springdrain trickle, no woods
at the far end of the dream where poems thundered
up like pheasants at my feet, or slipped,
like deer at evening, into fields, quieter
than stars coming out.—Lies, all lies.

There is only this close dark place, smelling
of chemicals, where I develop
images of a free-lancing eye. The negatives
frame emptiness, or sometimes the underside
of a table, a length of necktie, a jutting chin,
nostrils, a tilted room—as if an idiot
rolling on the floor had pointed a camera.

I wake again smelling diesel fuel,
for in the night my dreams have pounded past
like big trucks on the interstate going
through gears, pulling enigmatic freight.

1973

VASSAR MILLER

Caught In The Act

We ascertain your stone
Correctly set in place,
The grace around it grown
To an appropriate grace.

Such soft and senseless gestures
By persons of perspicience
Seemed all so many postures
For which you had no patience.

But even if you mock
We cannot catch your jeer
And here we will come back
To you who are not here.

(Or so you'd have it said,
All tidy in your shroud
Like a baby tucked in bed,
So proper and so proud.)

1962

Confession at a Friends' Meeting

Thoughts paddle in the floods of silence,
no single spar of sound to cling to,
except the rumble of my neighbor's belly,
the creaking of his shoes,

only my tears to serve as notes
upon the staff of unflawed air

for all the selves born, battered by
waters bearing none home.

Heart flails among those billows, washed
half away, uncentering down
in love, saying itself without
a word, singing past music.

1973

Domestication

Adam looked at the creature.
Rigid with fright,
"Beast," he whispered. "Tiger."
His limbs turned light.

Adam, thrust out of Eden,
found the strange air
poison till he learned to
call it despair.

Adam, eyes darkening,
cried out, "Whàt wolf . . . ?"
Death he named, and caged it
safe in himself.

1973

ROBERT MORGAN

Dark Corner

Was said around home nobody
lived in Dark Corner, just
near it. For us it was across
the ridge in South Carolina.
After dark when the wind was right
you could tell somebody was making.
Strong as the fermenting shade
under an apple tree
fumes came chimneying
through the gap in Painter
Mountain. Whole cornfields asweat
through an eye. What focus.
Not to mention sunlight gathered on the hillsides
by the flush of cornleaves, and ground water
freighting minerals taken by sucker
roots, long weeks of play
with hoe and cultivator before
the laying by; stalks stretching
exhilarate in the July night
till sun fills the cobs' teeth
with oil. No mention
of top cutting,
fodder pulling. Talk
of digestion in mash vats at the head
of the holler, sugar agitations,
transubstantiations, work
of bacterial excitements till
hot sweetness arrives. Comes the runoff
calling from the corruptions and burning
a ghost returned by the reflector
to a cool point. Manifests
heavy drops, pore
runny with lunar ink.

Back up under the summit line
where smoke is hid by haze
and updrafts lift
the mash smell a few
hundred yards out of state,
the lookout waits on the laurel ledge,
gun in lap to fire warning.
A rattler suns near, his crevice
high over the settlement.
Down there houses propped, a toilet
wades the creek on stilts. Man
here'll go down
on his daughter, god
damn her soul.

Uncle got sent up for moonshine,
did time in the Atlanta pen.
Long as water runs and corn grows green
and fire boils water I'll be making
Judge, reckon on it, he said.
But something there broke him.
Rumor blamed the whippings. He
came back old, a new man.

1974

HARRY MORRIS

At Loggerheads

Masked,
It perches, black eyes one with its domino,
Its verdict death and seeming hooded blind;
With those eyes blank, all mercy locked away.
No creature understands its sentences.
Yet it sees all things even the tunneling shrew,
Whose subterranean passes it looks upon,
Body motionless, head sweeping the field,
To turn its face from the safe but lift the doomed.
I have found upon barbed wire a young mole,
Useless forefeet widespread still to dig
Or pray; have found soft-bodied insects, left
From birth with no defense; found hard-shelled stag
Horn beetles, armor like pasteboard cloven, all
Protection vain, and once, just once, a snake,
Pathetic tiny evil crowned, *tantilla*
Coronata, pierced at the heart upon
A crown of thorn. Yea, butcher bird, your way
Inscrutable.

1972

NORMAN C. MOSER

The Song of April Riley

I sing, belatedly, of April Riley
whom I followed with the sun following me,
whose simple summery tresses in my fourteenth year
would entwine around me the sunset's purest pink bows.

Surely there were dimples like her two cherries,
riper apple breasts, cotton
silhouettes more full to reap.

But she was for me. She of the rippling loose limbs
dancing through her shyness like sun moving through clouds.
She with a colt's wry beginnings of grace.
Her tiny blue eyes had a sunset of her own in them.

More like, perhaps, a slim young pine,
she seemed, then, the sweetest magnolia tree
that ever blossomed under sultry Southern sun,
content to rest in the shade, peeping
out occasionally, a wintery, *subtle* sun,
secure like him in her circle, her power.

Pattering like a fieldmouse past the barn,
weaving gaily round rocks and trees,
I followed like a bear on the scent of deer,
and accepted without words the year's first grapes,
which, having picked herself, she held out haltingly to me.

Then mother's song "April!" winged out through the trees
on the sweetened air all the way down to the orchard.
We, we stopped shuffling around each other
like dogs around a bone or bees about honey.
Hadn't even flinched when I took hold of her,
a self-styled matador futilely grasping for horns,
but when I did no more she sailed shortly off
in answer to that other song. I didn't wait,
galloped off that instant in the opposite direction.

1965

PAUL BAKER NEWMAN

Formation

The flower is the column
budding into thought
the pollen of the body, the sun that is not the sun.

It is something light
springing like cognac
in the mind thinking of oranges
and wheat, like grass out of tile
roofs
          the wash like sunlight
in a goblet
high up in the sinuses smelling bitter
spikes of purple flowers
     dry and bitter
and formal
hot light on a beach
fine sparkling
     of thistles
flames of white patterning the dry gold wheat.

The flames of the light
like clear transparent sherry
searching their equivalent
                              in thought
the sunlight that is formed of sunlight
producing sunlight
     thick-walled olive leaves
translucent poppies
little waxy flowers
     drifting petals beneath the olive trees
dry dusty green columns out of the sword leaves
     budding
producing flowers.

1972   Manzanares

Routes

The body in the live sunlight
of the skin
        flows like leaves,
the fine fish of the eucalyptus,
through the olives.

The pleasure of the blood is
feeling its way toward recognitions, the same
as the pleasure of the cells, feeling
their own survival, recognizing
     the routes
through the air
through the water
     through the light
flying, swimming, leaping
like the trunks of eucalyptus, porpoises.

1972   Civitavecchia

July Fourth Weather

The night wind
comes with its rain of salt,
a ripple of green blue-berried cedar
sighing through the wind's teeth.
Steel grey the inlet widens
beyond the shoals, dark-
ening and turning silver,
long restless lines of break-
ers wash the dark grey sand
with overlapping planes of
cloudy silver, where the sea oats
nod their harsh plaited seeds.

1966

PRESTON NEWMAN

Gen. Sideburn

Gen. Sideburn was a pisspoor military tactician, so poor that,
after he got whipped at First Bull Run, his adversary, Gen.
Jubal Early, could have swaggered into the White House smoking
segars and cussing like a mountaineer from Franklin County, Va.;
in fact, he could have played footsie with Mary Todd Lincoln;
but (deep down) Jubal felt insecure, timid, frustrated; so he
effected a strategic retreat from Washington, D.C., and regrouped
himself.

But back to Gen. Sideburn: he and his rattled batallions got shat
upon, successively, at Cold Harbor,
                            Fredericksburg,
                            the Wilderness:
and Sideburn just kept bumbling on, letting his burnsides grow,
until Gen. Meade politely suggested a courtmartial: the verdict:
Sideburn found "answerable for the want of success."

Success at what? These nowadays Grant and his Bottle,
                            Lee and Traveller,
                            Jackson, his Lemons and
                            Bible

seem faint and longgone, but young Ambrose Everett Sideburn
lives next door, his cheekwhiskers no less immortal than Pres.
Lincoln's Mole carved in granite on Mount Rushmore by John
Gutson de la Mothe Borglum, who, as revealed in his photos,
was also
                            bushfaced.

1971

JOHN NIXON, JR.

Miss Maggie and the Voices

On anybody's roster of old girls
Not readily forgotten in our town,
Miss Maggie's name is tall. When she came down

From her last bristling day at the switchboard,
Her business frown still on her, she was through
Forever with wrong numbers and the new

Dumb operators, through with thirty years
Of disembodied voices that barked, purred,
Shouted, or whined. Lord, what she *had* endured.

Good-by. Good riddance. So Miss Maggie walked,
Idle and ponderous, around the square.
With high-topped shoes on, with her faded hair

Mannishly bobbed, she had clumped forth at last
To face the voices. I can see her yet,
Pausing immensely in a tangled street—

Propped on her cane, letting the traffic swerve,
Miss Maggie, scowling, whom the voices made
Leathery, acid, lonely, and unafraid.

1962

LINDA PASTAN

Drift

Lying in bed this morning
you read to me of continental drift,
how Africa and South America
sleeping once side by side
slowly slid apart;
how California even now
pushes off like a swimmer
from the country's edge, along
the San Andreas Fault.
And I thought about you and me
who move in sleep each night
to the far reaches of the bed,
ranges of blanket between us.
It is a natural law this drift
and though we break it
as we break bread
over and over again, you remain
Africa with your deep shade,
your heat. And I, like California,
push off from your side
my two feet cold
against your back, dreaming
of Asia Minor.

1974

LOUIS PHILLIPS

When the Dolphins Came

We were alive, stalled at the heart,
    air made
dungeons of regret,
    but when the dolphins came
to make a merriment of sea,
    snub-nosed,
       goose-beaked,

& flung their dolting selves
    moon-like
to a spray, the enamoured arm
    of the ocean
thickened before our bow,
    & everywhere
      was dolphin,

sea-people of fleshly tongue,
    bark & whistle
of a snapped world below us.
    A naturalist
had spied
    such creatures
      in Brazil,

had marvelled as they
    lolloped through trees
"with modified
    mammalian gallop."
Now Arion's music
    toppled us
      with surge,

Commotion of lidded eye.
    The dense world,
Torpedo-shaped,

                   rose less easily
        than they. O when I die,
                   let me be,
                        or let me be

        with dolphins, our hard bodies
                   resurrecting
        goodness everywhere,
                   leaping single-filed
        swayed or reckoned
                   like faith itself,
                        or if I drown,

        My love, in love, be temperate
                   & push me
        toward the shore. But here,
                   unlike Brazil,
        or any of the mortal world,
                   here the ocean
                        was a tree,

        immense, & all our sorrows fell
                   loosely-veined,
        fretted to a high horizon,
                   went thrashing,
        their high-falcated fins
                   barely
                        out of sight.

        1974

Southern Canine

Bells on the hills
in the blue woods of winter
hounds run
all night.

Days, they lie heavy in dust,
awaiting a scratching at
their hides, a scent
fainting forward
deeper, upcountry.
They wait for the dark.

Nobody notices them
except when a pack in heat
raises hell
thru a shopping center

or headlights hit the ditch
where the hounds
have landed
massacred by cars.

1965

STANLEY PLUMLY

Silt

The truth is that we are all potential
fossils still carrying within our bodies
the crudities of former existences.
—Loren Eiseley

On the underside of the skin,
on the thin chalk walls
the birdtracks in the snow,
the intaglio of ferns,
the blood shedding
its leaves
(the mind as large as the Paleocene,
echoing each liquid,
sucking step),

on this underflesh,
fossilized,
white as wet cement—
dinosaurs with wings
flying like hell
below water
to finally break air
on the beaches of fingernails—

on these coral reefs
ascending like skyscrapers
to the world,
on this star of flesh,
hammered by all bodies
to transparency,
each heart, hand, foot
and fingerprint.

1971

That Summer

That summer when the creeks all dried up
Except for a few deep holes
Under the caved-out roots of oaks
Now leaning toward the water's edge.
The catfish clung to the mud,
But now and then a perch was caught
In the oatsack seine.
Even the Tar was a trickle,
And I could walk all the way across
On the rocks. The place
Where we had swung from limb to water,
Splashing below surface and rising sputtering,
Was now just mud
From which a turtle crawled.
> They sat on the porches
> And talked of the weather
> And Herbert Hoover,
> Cursing both and every son of a bitch
> Who had voted for him.
> Even if the Baptists saved any souls
> Worth the saving
> Where in the hell would they find
> Enough water to baptize them?
A wild turkey flew out of the woods.
It was out of season, but it fed
The family for two days.
It tasted better than the turtle
That looked like mud and tasted like mud.

1970

PAUL RAMSEY

In an Ordinary Place

If you think too long, the very bricks cry out against you.
They cry of fire whirling within them. Their speech is a
        redness.
If a flame blackens them, the flame speaks of their nature.
If they stand in a wall, mortar does not tame them.
Feel them. Roughen your hands against the uneven surface.
The roughness you feel is not the roughness of your feelings:
        it is the roughness of bricks.
Crying out against you. Crying out for you
That you also, like the far birds which are sparrows,
May move out of your thought into the wide stand of
        landscape,
Grey lights of hue, green on yellow transcending itself,
Foreign of sound, wild of bird thicketing, clean of space.
If you deny your vision, the very bark of the trees will hold
        you off
Which offered to you, correctly, the feel of existence,
A shape prior to the essence of your withdrawal.
Let red blaze on red! It is a day good for looking.
Should you fashion a wall, fashion it with your own hands,
Brick on brick, delicately mortared, stronger than the wind's
        zest,
Capable of surrounding a place of meditation.
Then you may think there. But not too long, lest the wall
        wall you,
Lest you fail to hear the very stones of their speaking.

1964

A Snowman in March

He is a sort of god.
Where slowly, dense, and cool
The deep lawn of snow thaws,
This craggy snowman, odd
As a trick of eye, stands,
Capricious as applause,
Idle martyr and fool,
With head half gone, no hands.
The seeds await his nod.

1965

Epitaph Spoken by a Former Lover

If many bodies were her guest,
She bore them lightly. They are gone,
And small impression leave they here
On this slight body stiff with rest.
Her breasts are now become a stone.
Fitly. They have the earth to bear
As we, her lovers, have the sun.

1965

A Reply to
Donald Justice's Southern Gothic

Sick roses fall, in spite of our intent
To tie them on their stems with bits of string.
Our hands may bleed a little, even yet,
On some stray thorn athwart the garden path
Or we may stumble in the matted weeds
And nearly fall, or hear in silence songs,
Mere ghosts of songs some jay or fiddler sung,
But most is past, the gate is open wide,
The wood quite rotted out that held us in.
Therefore our freedom is our being now
And being is the merely going forth.
The trellises you dressed with careful art,
That you for years have made to bloom and bloom
In miracle of fragrance from dead seed
(My rougher hands have patched a post or two)
Must be forgot until they fall to dust
With house and land and loved and hated kin,
Till dust is all that's left, and none to see
What comes of dust. What could be freer then?

1962

JULIA RANDALL

Crazy Jane on Her Birthday

after WBY

How many times have I been born?
Said Crazy Jane.
Once of woman, once of man.
The births of generation
Are one, said Jane.

You have died, the Bishop said, you have died
Wherever you have lain
For pleasure or for livelihood
Beside a paying man.

Oh you are right, and I am right,
But righter than us all
Love's fading foot upon the stair
That takes a soul to hell.

I stood up in my skin and wept
Before great Hades' crown,
And I looked back, said Crazy Jane,
Upon my own lost man.

And on that day I bore a song
That turned the beasts to kind.
All nature but the heart of man
Took supper at my hand.

But man has torn my heart in two,
And by the half of stone
I perished once, said Crazy Jane.
On that day I was born.

1966

The Dappled Ponies

When dappled ponies gobbled roses from the hedges
and cobwebs hung spread-eagled from the wires
dew-clotted innocent of victim bait or spider

When morning ran the mists out of the valley
and all the little suns were coming up at once
                    over the mountain

Then I remember steam from kneeling cattle
rising in mushroom puffs above their heads
the fierce horns the sweet and holy haloes
the heavy beasts all born again
                    reincarnated saints

Saint Angus and Saint Brahmin a bull
named Gabriel rose like a martyr a wreath
of tenderness around his head
                    and knelt again sighing

Saints live long but dew is swift in drying

If grace is sought I think about the valley
nurturing its nectarines and honey
the ponies nibbling roses from the hedges

The dappled ponies with their saddles squeaking

1972

Headstone of Fire

When father died, I burned his holy bibles.
Dozens of bibles, like a burning bush,
Blazed upward in one vast, voluminous rush
Of holy characters, tongues of flaming titles.

Like Moses on the mountain side, I stood
Dumb-smitten at the bush, hearing I AM
THAT I AM, seeing the glorious anagrams
Of God swirling through the darkening woods.

Those holy characters in their furnace of fire
Walked round unsinged: Adam before the fall,
Isaiah purged by coals, the Lord in all
Transfigurations, David at the lyre.

What prompted me at dusk to tend that flame?
Was I the priest of Baal, hardened of heart?
Or was that fire a pillar raised by art
For one whose tongue strove with God's holy name?

1971

GIBBONS RUARK

Sleeping Out with My Father

Sweet smell of earth and easy rain on
Canvas, small breath fogging up the lantern
Glass, and sleep sifting my bones, drifting me
Far from hide-and-seek in tangled hedges,
The chicken dinner with its hills of rice
And gravy and its endless prayers for peace,
Old ladies high above me creaking in the choir loft,
And then the dream of bombs breaks up my sleep,
The long planes screaming down the midnight
Till the whistles peel my skin back, the bombs
Shake up the night in a sea of lightning
And stench and spitting shrapnel and children
Broken in the grass, and I am running
Running with my father through the hedges
Down the flaming streets to fields of darkness,
To sleep in sweat and wake to news of war.

1970

Aboard the Liner (II)

Adrift, I float through invisible barriers,
Illicitly penetrating First—
No one stops me; like the fog I move
Across the sinking carpets, past the bars
Of elegance, through lounges deep with plush
As if I knew the way. Stewards glance
Through me, and jeweled wives ignore
The interloper's gall. I gaze through mists
That tremble out of Tourist Class, enveloping
The statues, fountains, curving gold of stairs.
Beyond the vapors, the stars pavane, while lost
Beneath the layers of old vibrations, cashmered
Passengers ponder charts, guess the depth of seas.

1973

The Sons

There was great relief at his funeral.
We had all murdered him with promises
Of love, and no one had caught us—
The perfect crime, we thought, feeling
Our new identities like holy robes.
Mother was so radiant in black—
Reborn (we thought), an earnest of our
Immortality; she would grace us
Into heaven, pleading pardon for
Our sins. Her look of grief would pass.
                                        Too soon
The cortege fled—the bearers paid, the flowers
Shrinking into the grave. And suddenly

The magic of death was over—only the mound
Remained, like a ground swell in the earth,
A throb in nature. And as we turned to go,
Mother looked much older. Her breasts were gone,
Her face a warp behind the veil. She fell
Upon his clay, whispering (we thought)
The promises.
           Then we heard the curse.

1965

Desideratum

I search always for a room
    in which all things matter greatly
        and equally:

To enter which I leave outside
    the isotropic door all manner of instruments
        of calibration,

All gyres and springes, all traps
    and pitfalls inherent in the nature
        of measurement,

Except the catoptric glass
    a man needs for mirroring the image
        of his own serenity:

That caprifig hung in the slow,
    reluctant branches to hasten the flowers
        to willingness,

Perfumed catalyst charming
    the wasp to work its flickering,
        fiddling charm:

That is, the whole heart,
    honest as the equiparent fullness
        of the emptiest

Habitational dream:
    for across that threshold is love,
        that perfectly pure space

Where no dimensions are given.
    Bodies are not needed to describe
        the things in that room,

From the shelves and ledges
    of which is reflected only the amiable,
        and uncritical, soul.

1974

JAMES SEAY

The Tree Man
at the Parthenon Tourist

Probably once a month
I see his truck of trees
parked overnight at the tourist home
and I wonder what brings him there.
Most of the big truckers
keep on trucking.
I want to think it has to do
with all the elephant ears,
not the replica of the Parthenon
down the street.
I want to see him one summer evening,
the tree man, sitting out on the porch
with the proprietress, dreaming
the one rain forest in Nashville.
But that can't be the only reason.
I called the lady and she said
she has to take them in
when the first frost falls.
And in the basement they die off
for the winter.
What about those bare months, tree man?
All your greenwood trees
are for the new rich in Chattanooga or Atlanta.
Is it that she's promised to take you down
to where the whole elephant walks,
and on into that secret graveyard
all the white hunters dream of?
Or are you trying, tree man,
to remember something forever?

1974

The Soldier and the Singer

(metaphor 204)

Down there one night by the low bush squatting
Two days before he died
My friend charmed my wife and me

Hands gesturing like pale flags shaking
Telling us tales of the Sargosso Sea,
Japs in caves,
The bon vivante in Russian ports—then,
"Hear, hear, listen,"
As the bush between his words produced a mockingbird.
And again and again he had us listen
And there he marveled us
As at his trembled hand the bird sang.

Down there one night by the low bush squatting
The Sargosso Sea,
Japs in caves,
Russian ports,
And the hauntingest song in a dark dust never to be repeated.

Down there one night by the low bush squatting
He sang to us with his palely gesturing hand
His death, laughing gently halfway between war and bush
As if he grew weak and impatient for his own failing,
Anxious for the dark lark song tipped now sudden at his
        fingers.

Down there one night by the low bush squatting
Two days before he died
Such dust, death, song, such splendid quaking.

1965

DAVE SMITH

The Cold Comes On

This was the season you loved
with the cold coming
like mist or lace
in the jacked-up rows
of hairy peanuts.
When you were a child
we walked out like this
and they marched, those cones,
beside us like bandoliered soldiers
shaking the snow off their chests.
We remember how the snap
of dead slivers of wood
turned into bullets
under our feet.
The squirrels still strut
out on their meager ridges
to scan our mustered troops
and the field lies as it always has.
Today the plowing ends, the digging's done.
The field swallows the dead soldiers
as we see it for what it is, a tool,
a source of dank beginnings, a life
of withered endings. Cold comes
and there is snow sealing off
the sky where the smoke
from your mother's oven
breaks up on the huddling trees.
Dead. Very well, everything dies.
We accept this, you understand.
But the cold is coming on, the season
you always loved and we must go back.
We are very old. We stumble on furrows
We cannot survive the nights in this field.

1971

Snake Sermon

In this picture you will see
Big Stone Gap, Virginia, the white
petals of dogwood blurred back
of the woman standing in what
we call the nave. She lifts
the snake, a moccasin, mouth pure
as cream when it opens, the shade
of Daddy's inner thigh. It ought
to be a rattler, big diamonds
chaining her throat like beads,
a tail to shake hell out of those
windows that overlook nothing.
But it's only black, thick
as horse cock in her little fingers,
its tongue licking the silence
out of the rough pews. You can't
buy rattlers anymore, big dozers
drove them away to prairies and
the snatching hands of farm boys
in sweat-belted baseball hats.
Times change, even way in here.
One cottonmouth per Sunday, now,
bless the Lord for his bounty.
Three for Easter and Christmas.

1974

FRANK STEELE

Being Sketched by a Friend

"Be still," she says
But in her eyes you can feel yourself
Going away as she works
From across the kitchen table.
Talking and laughing, she puts you down
On paper, piece by piece. The chin,
The nose, a cheek, one blank
Eye, as if they were being barbered,
All feel the soft brush of her look
Pass by and take them

Out of afternoon, out of the kitchen
Beyond the window where you see
A bulldozer crew at the foot of a hill
A quarter mile away. A crane wheeling
Over there claws, scoops into the earth,
Lifts, swings, settles, shakes
Itself off. Its roar is pillowed on glass.
Up the hill a few cows, undisturbed,
Move around in the sun, losing weight

Grown light at this distance, as a man
Half asleep sheds husks of fatigue,
A snakeskin of himself onto the bed
Feeling the scales drop away
That no one sees.
                          These she catches,
Sketches, secrets in a man's life
Told this once as you work to be still.
Almost without being touched, the part
Of yourself that takes up space

Grows buoyant as you float to her
Corklike, undesired, and in strange waters.
She looks down where her fingers move
Getting it right. The crane, half hidden
By its mounds, is still, its hole stopped
With shadows. Late sunlight has climbed up the slope
And this moment, once only, the cows
Are walking on water.

1969

To Laura Phelan: 1880-1906

Drunk I have been. And drunk I was that night
I lugged your stone across the other graves,
to set you up a hundred yards away.
Flowers I found, then. Drunk I have been.
And am, standing here with no moon to spill
on the letters of your name; my loud fingers
feeling them out. The stone is mossed over.
And why must I bring myself in the dark
to stand here among the sour grasses
that stain my white jeans? Drunk I have been.
See, the thick dew slides on the trees, wet weeds,
wetness smears the air; and a vague surf
of wildflowers pushes my feet, slipping
close to my legs. When the thought comes at last
that people fall apart, that the things we do
will not do. Ends. Then, we come to scenes
like this. This scene of you. You apart:
this is not you; and yet, this is where I stand
and close my eyes, and feel the ragged wind
blow red and maul my hair. In the night somewhere,
dandelions foam. This is not you. Drunk
I have been. Across this graveyard, that
is where you are. Yet I stand here. Would ask
things of your name. Would wish. Would not be told
of the stink in the skull, the eye's collapse.
Would be told something new, something unknown.—
A mosquito bites my hand. The only sound
is the rough wind. Drunk I have been,
here, at the loam's maw, before this stone
of yours, which is not you. Which is.

1971

JOHN STONE

To a 14 Year Old Girl
in Labor and Delivery

I cannot say it to you, Mother. Child.
Nowhere now is there a trace of the guile
that brought you here. Near the end of exile

I hold you prisoner, jailer, in my cage—
with no easy remedy for your rage
against him and the child. Your coming of age

is a time of first things: a slipping of latches;
of parallels like fire and the smell of matches.
The salmon swims upstream. The egg hatches.

1971

Resuscitation

When the heart coughed
and the lungs folded
like flowers
your eyes had barely closed.

By all signs and proper science
you were dead

warm and dying
in one unmerciful
and unelectric instant.

Sweat hung
in my eyebrows
like a father's.

It is easier now
to reconstruct
your death in life.

How four days later
as you play at trains

I can remember
when the blood began
to bump like box-cars
in the back of your eyes,

1971

The Babysitter

watching children
   leap to her excitement, tiny fish
breaking the smooth, the safe;

my fish (old shark, heavy in its leaden sleep)
arises, sensing flesh
   and possibility

leaning down to catch their hands
                       (creatures
of the womb I ploughed),
her blouse white in the sun

the waves
surge over rocks exposed
by laws involving
passing ships

         I slide
into the comfort
of imagined rape
remembering how first
it was, how bad,
then torpid nights
riding the great swells far from land—
eyes, asking *why?*
scratch mine with coral—
shallow water,
           deadly reefs. . . .

1968

The Warehouse Chute

As a boy I started at the top,
Sixth floor, as high as my father's business
Reached, a sort of skyline
In a squat and stolid city
Where men moved among goods, and knew
Themselves as the goods moved, always down.
But that was their concern
And none of my business.
Seated on cardboard or wax paper
I spiralled that metal slide
Past every merchandise
At jerkneck speed, and didn't care
If I never stopped, because
I knew I would—come to the smooth
Bright easy finish of that ride.

I never needed Virgil
Or thought of him, but now
That place seems hell enough—
A house of wares which never spoke
A word, or sang a song,
Yet held its men, my father
And his father, as a sorcerer
Enthralls a knight,
Benights an age, held them
And made them move
As it would have them move
In darkness and in circles
Wearing them empty as that chute—
Seems hell enough.
Now in my dreams the spiral
Spirals without end.
I see myself on every level
Smiled at by a carton,
Never Beatrice, smiled at
By this past that hands me on,
Guideless, always going down.

1965

HOLLIS SUMMERS

The Foundry: Lost Wax Casting

In sculpture all the words mean.
I followed all the directions.
I made a figure out of wax.
I encased it in a mold
After the manner of art
Made from the waste from somebody else's mind;
Luto, they call it, the people who write books,
A fine word for making you feel like Orpheus.

Luto, sand, plaster,
Chicken wire around the wax
An inch inside the outside world;
I followed all the directions
Trying not to think of chickens,
Fitting a system of sprues, runners, vents,
Investing:
Invest, that's the word.

It means to adorn, cover, furnish,
Install with ceremony;
It also means to spend and to besiege.
The wax melts out of the investment.
We must leave space for bronze.
The space is the bad of life
The good of art, burned out like memory.
The bronze we poured was fire colored.

I thought I had fashioned a bird
Soaring as chickens cannot soar.
In the bronze the bird has not flown.
But somewhere the fire bronze soars.

2.
Maybe painting pictures and shaping statues
Mean idolatry; maybe Mohammed was right;
Maybe we should stick to geometry, endless arabesques,
Repeating calligraphy into infinity.

But I am suspicious of the many syllabled words.
I trust a bird, a tree, a girl,
A bare foot on the grass,
More than I trust a proclaiming rug.

Mattering words are statues and colored figures anyhow,
All idols, facing Mecca;
Perhaps idolatry is our final goal,
Seeking God through images.

I would say a noun and a verb;
I would make a naked human figure; I would pour bronze.

1974

ELEANOR ROSS TAYLOR

Song

Don't go to sleep! I begged.
But a child pulling grass
Under the tamaracks
Could not know the wear of the field.
In your sleeping face
There was nothing to show
That you remembered me, or cared,
Or would come back.

Don't go to sleep! I cry,
Now gray—but can I know
The stupefaction of all losses
In your stone face
Where nothing shows
If you remember me, or care,
Or will come back.

1970

The Flying Change

1.

The canter has two stride patterns, one on the right
lead and one on the left, each a mirror image of the
other. The leading foreleg is the last to touch the
ground before the moment of suspension in the air.
On cantered curves, the horse tends to lead with the
inside leg. Turning at liberty, he can change leads
without effort during the moment of suspension, but
a rider's weight makes this more difficult. The aim
of teaching a horse to move beneath you is to remind
him how he moved when he was free.

2.

A single leaf turns sideways in the wind
in time to save a remnant of the day;
I am lifted like a whipcrack to the moves
I studied on that barbered stretch of ground,
before I schooled myself to drift away

from skills I still possess, but must outlive.
Sometimes when I cup water in my hands
and watch it slip away and disappear,
I see that age will make my hands a sieve;
but for a moment the shifting world suspends

its flight and leans toward the sun once more,
as if to interrupt its mindless plunge
through works and days that will not come again.
I hold myself immobile in bright air,
sustained in time astride the flying change.

1974

WILLIAM E. TAYLOR

Down Here with Aphrodite

The skies are hung in sex,
the air in bougainvillia
sweet and pregnant as the ocean.

I have lived and burned on her beaches
where heart and soul are attacked
by coitus.

Ah, love
I enter the expressway
to your silky
florida,
copper-toned and drowned
in orange juice.

Your lips wilt like poinsettias
after the christmas freeze of my coming.

Spanish bayonets also thrive here.
Their blades drink the wind.
Wounds heal slow,

but in Florida
blood throbs hard
to an immortal
erection.

1966

On Sundays We All Sat Around and Just Looked at One Another

The orange trees are threadbare
by a sudden 24-hour freeze.

That's the way with winter in Florida.

Not the snow my grandfather knew
in his fruit market in Newark, New Jersey
the cold gold chain looped across his vest
gray bristles frost on his New England lip,
and Grandmother in the parlor
counting her money.

Grandfather finally made a fortune
selling Florida oranges and real estate
and didn't worry so much about the weather.

Later, Mother, in high southern style,
spent every shining dime.

1965

The Jolly Rapist

Mr. Bunch, the jolly rapist,
    A man of radical views,
Appeared one night to our surprise
    On the six o'clock news.

"I'm your friendly dirty old man,
    To youth and gaity prone,"
He said and stared with his beady eyes
    Into the microphone.

"You think perhaps I deserve these cuffs
        For the crimes that I have wrought,
But you'd never have guessed the man I am
        If I hadn't been caught."

Mr. Bunch, Mr. Bunch,
        What man are you indeed?
"I'm your jolly rapist, lads,
        And that is all my creed."

"I'd rather not prosecute,"
        Said the offended flirt,
"Mr. Bunch is so jolly and sweet,
        And besides, it didn't hurt."

It's all in how you look at things
        Whether they're loved or hated.
Mr. Bunch put up a sign,
        "Rape, Incorporated."

Citizens of the American Age,
        Do ye in this wise:
Reward men of spirit and grit
        And men of enterprise.

1972

The Temptress

Bored, she spoke without articulate speech
To the animal in man she said she hated,
Calling, calling the beast to the barred door
With woman scent, covered in rich colors
To show that inside she is succulent,
The inside she so detests and loves because
It's all she thinks she is.

Stretching, yawning in leopard style herself,
Staring with empty eyes,
Long nailed fingers opening, shutting like claws,
She shakes her head as if she had a mane,
Instructs the barred beast in intricacies of locks.

Then the animal would spring, leap to her
And she would whip it back. "Man, man," she cries,
"Lock up your beast."

The more intricate the locks man made for his cage
The more delight she felt in uncaging him.
"Look, look," her pacing said,
"All men have an animal ready to eat me."

Just when her boredom was overcome with fear
The fear departed.
"No man has an animal in a cage,
The animal ate the man, and I uncage the beast
And drive it back in anger."

1966

The Metaphysician

Smoke he blew curled above his wife,
A milky way in bed. Outside
Their window and a branch, the night
Curled too. A question mark. He thought,
"The Universe is curls." Smoke gone,
His cigarette mashed out, his mind
Was punctuated with doubt. The shade
He pulled blanked out all curls, all questions
Of night. The universe is not,
Is nothing he knew. But in sleep
He dreamt of Noah's ark and waked.
The emptiness is full, he felt.
And felt that he was curling up,
A mindless question of the flesh.
He reached . . . surprised his wife was there.
From the silent nothing, a black
High silk empty hat, a rabbit
Jumped. And so beasts disembarked
Upon the shore. In morning light
All furniture of life swam back:
He tore a plum from the window tree,
And ate his heart, the quack.

1966

Intimations of Immorality

Married five years. The surfeit has increased:
we're living on the leavings of the feast.
Too long familiar with each other's bed,
for strangers we would have fresh maidenhead.

I, without Shelley's adolescent gift
of selfishness, can't bear to make the rift
in the weak fabric of our makebelieve.
I blame tradition. Starting out with Eve
the West has crowned the bridal night, forgot
the rest, and left the lovers there to rot.
While wiser China brings the bridal pair
strangers to bed and keeps their secret there,
restrained by day to mutual courtesy,
love flowers late.
                              No use to you and me,
this wisdom. There's a player's saying fit:
Love needs a third act. Marriage isn't it.

1972

JAMES WHITEHEAD

He Remembers Figuring a Logic for the Life That Went on the Summers He Cruised Timber

One time a wildcat jumped from a tree, and once
We saw twelve snakes in a single day of work,
But mostly there was little more than the dance
Of flying insects from the sun—then back
To Woodville for a sorry meal and beer
And waitresses who loved the picture show
And probably a screw without much cheer.
I tried to understand what I should know.

I thought of phrases. *Natural weather* was one.
A slow mean life was another. Also *bad taste.*

Late at night the sun stayed on my skin
And the motel sheets were stiff, and my smoke was a waste
Unless by force of mind I figured breath
Goes back to the woods, rounding out my death.

1973

About a Year
After He Got Married
He Would Sit Alone
in an Abandoned Shack
in a Cotton Field
Enjoying Himself

I'd sit inside the abandoned shack all morning
Being sensitive, a fair thing to do
At twenty-three, my first son born, and burning
To get my wife again. The world was new
And I was nervous and wonderfully depressed.

The light on the cotton flowers and the child
Asleep at home was marvelous and blessed,
And the dust in the abandoned air was mild
As sentimental poverty. I'd scan
Or draw the ragged wall the morning long.

Newspaper for wallpaper sang but didn't mean.
Hard thoughts of justice were beyond my ken.
Lord, forgive young men their gentle pain,
Then bring them stones. Bring their play to ruin.

1973

MILLER WILLIAMS

How, Having Given Up the Classical Temper for the Romantic, We Try to Find Meaning in Death

It's hard to think the brain
a ball of ropey dough
should have posited pain
or come to know

how to distinguish legend
from life and let it go
and think we live, and imagine
that makes it so.

If these are things we lend
a fragile credence to
we come to comprehend
or think we do

how something which has the skill
to think of the mouth kissed
should lose the words and will
and not exist

or look at itself astonished
as it does now, and know
all things are good and honest
as this is so.

1974

EMILY HERRING WILSON

Down Zion's Alley

Down Zion's Alley, off First Street,
Shacks rub their crippled backs
Against the white man's fence.
When it rains, the floods wash trash
All the way to his dreams.
He sits up in bed, calls out,
"Something's dead in the alley."
And turns out the light.
The sun sucks up the night,
Leaving the shacks bare, clean,
The fenced yards full of their seeds.

1970

CHARLES WRIGHT

Hardin County
—CPW, 1904-1972

There are birds that are parts of speech, bones
That are suns in the quick earth.
There are ice floes that die of cold.
There are rivers with many doors, and names
That pull their thread from their own skins.
Your grief was something like this.

Or self-pity, I might add, as you did
When you were afraid to sleep,
And not sleep, afraid to touch your bare palm;
Afraid of the wooden dog, the rose
Bleating beside your night stand; afraid
Of the slur in the May wind.

It wasn't always like that, not in those first years
When the moon went on without its waters,
When the cores blew out of their graves in Hardin County.
How useless it is to cry out, to try
And track that light, now
Reduced to a grain of salt in the salt snow.

I want the dirt to go loose, the east wind
To pivot and fold like a string.
I want the pencil to eat its words,
The star to be sucked through its black hole.
And everything stays the same,
Locks unpicked, shavings unswept on the stone floor.

The grass reissues its green music; the leaves
Of the sassafras tree take it and pass it on;
The sunlight scatters its small change.
The dew falls, the birds smudge on their limbs.
And, over Oak Hill, the clouds, those mansions of nothingness,
Keep to their own appointments, and hurry by.

1974

Old Baggage

These are the clothes I sent ahead to meet me.
I claim them at the depot like the next of kin
called to the morgue. Yes, yes, it is he.
Are these his personal effects? Yes, sign here.
I should never have sent them. Shed is shed.
All along the bypaths from all wars
Are strewn the web belts, gasmasks, and canteens
of those deserting to another life. No one demands
the damned detritus posted after him.
Drawing them on, I am caught in their old
folds and wrinkles. They have my harried smell
and fit convictingly. Now I must recognize
myself before the running. Yes, yes, it is I
was there, and I did all those things
there in that tangled time and in this clothing.

1974

CONTRIBUTORS

BETTY ADCOCK has published poems in *Nation, Poetry Northwest, Chicago Review, New American Review,* and other magazines. Her first collection is forthcoming from Louisiana State University Press in 1975.

A. R. AMMONS, born in Whiteville, North Carolina, is now a professor at Cornell University and has published six volumes of poetry. His *Collected Poems* won the National Book Award in 1973.

JAMES APPLEWHITE, a native North Carolinian, is poet-in-residence at Duke University. He has published poems in *Harper's, New American Review,* and *Poetry;* the University of Georgia Press will publish his first collection of poems.

PRENTICE BAKER, from Louisville, Kentucky, is the author of a book of poems entitled *Down Cellar.*

COLEMAN BARKS is a Tennessee-born poet now teaching at the University of Georgia. His poems have appeared in *Red Clay Reader, Carolina Quarterly,* and other journals. He has published a collection entitled *The Juice,* Harper and Row, 1972.

GERALD W. BARRAX teaches English at North Carolina State University. His first collection of poetry, *Another Kind of Rain,* was published by the University of Pittsburgh Press in 1970.

SCOTT BATES teaches in the French Department at the University of the South and is currently editing a collection of poems on ecology. He is author of a critical study on Guillaume Apollinaire and editor of *Poems of War Resistance: 2300 B.C. to the Present.*

D. C. BERRY teaches creative writing at the University of Southern Mississippi and is an editor of *Mississippi Review.* His first collection is *Saigon Cemetery,* from the University of Georgia Press.

WENDELL BERRY of Port Royal, Kentucky, is widely known both as a poet and as a novelist. Among his recent collections are *Farming: A Hand Book* and *The Country of Marriages.*

DORIS BETTS teaches creative writing at The University of North Carolina at Chapel Hill. She has published six books of fiction; her most recent novel is *The Road to Pickle Beach*.

VAN K. BROCK teaches at Florida State University in Tallahassee. His poems have been published in the Borestone Mountain Poetry Award's *Best Poems of 1971, New Voices in American Poetry*, and *The New Yorker Book of Poetry*. His first collection is entitled *Final Belief*.

CATHARINE SAVAGE BROSMAN of Louisiana is the author of *Watering*, published by the University of Georgia Press.

TURNER CASSITY was born in Jackson, Mississippi, and now lives in Atlanta. His two collections of poetry are *Watchboy, What of the Night?* and *Steeplejacks in Babel*.

FRED CHAPPELL teaches creative writing at The University of North Carolina at Greensboro. He has published four novels and a recent collection of poetry, *The World Between the Eyes*, from Louisiana State University Press.

JAMES DICKEY, currently writer-in-residence at the University of South Carolina, is the author of eight books of poems and of *Deliverance*, a novel. His *Poems, 1957-1967* won the National Book Award.

R. H. W. DILLARD is a Virginia poet who teaches at Hollins College. His volumes of poetry are *The Day I Stopped Dreaming about Barbara Steele, News of the Nile*, and *After Borges*.

GERALD DUFF, born in Beaumont, Texas, has spent most of his life in East Texas and in Tennessee, but is now teaching at Kenyon College. He has published poems in a number of magazines and has completed a first collection, *The Deep Breather*.

CHARLES EDWARD EATON, a native of Winston-Salem, North Carolina, has published five volumes of poetry and two collections of short stories. His most recent volume of poetry is *On the Edge of the Knife*, 1970, and his sixth collection, *The Man in the Green Chair*, was the recipient of the Alice Fay di Castagnola Award from the Poetry Society of America in 1974.

JULIA FIELDS is the author of *Poems* and the recently published *East of Moonlight*, from Red Clay Books. Born in Alabama, she has been living and teaching in North Carolina.

GEORGE GARRETT has published four volumes of poetry and three novels. His most recent book of poems is *For a Bitter Season: New and Selected Poems.*

MALCOLM GLASS is a native Floridian now teaching at Austin Peay State University in Clarksville, Tennessee. His poems have appeared in *Mississippi Review, Appalachian Journal,* and *Southern Humanities Review.*

JOHN HAINES is a Virginian who homesteaded in Alaska for over a decade and is currently visiting professor at the University of Washington. Among his four books are *Winter News* and *Leaves and Ashes.*

O. B. HARDISON, director of the Folger Shakespeare Library, is the author or editor of numerous scholarly books. His collection of poems is entitled *Lyrics and Elegies* and was published by Scribner's in 1958.

WILLIAM HARMON is chairman of the English Department of The University of North Carolina at Chapel Hill and has published two books of poetry from Wesleyan University Press; the latest is *Legion: Civic Choruses.*

EUGENE HOLLAHAN, born in Tennessee, is now teaching courses in the novel at Georgia State University. He has published numerous poems and articles.

JOSEPHINE JACOBSEN, from Maryland, is a widely published poet. She has served two terms, 1971-73, as Consultant in Poetry to the Library of Congress. At present Mrs. Jacobsen is Honorary Consultant in American Letters to the Library of Congress. She has published four books of poetry; her fourth, *New and Selected Poems,* was published by Doubleday in 1974.

RODERICK JELLEMA teaches at the University of Maryland and has published poems in *Poetry Northwest, Dryad, New Republic,* and the *American Literary Anthology.* His collection of poems, *Something Tugging the Line,* was published by Dryad Press in 1974.

DONALD JUSTICE is a poet from Florida presently teaching in the Writers Workshop at Iowa. His books are *The Summer Anniversaries, Night Light,* and *Departures.*

DAVID MADDEN, from Kentucky, is the author of a collection of stories and four novels, including *Bijou*.

ADRIANNE MARCUS, a native of Fayetteville, North Carolina, is teaching in California and has just completed a book of poems entitled *Hologram*. Her first collection was *The Moon Is a Marrying Eye*.

HEATHER MILLER, now of Badin, North Carolina, has published three novels and two collections of poetry, *The Wind Southerly* and *Horse, Horse, Tyger, Tyger*, a Red Clay book.

JIM MILLER is a native of North Carolina now teaching at Western Kentucky University. Among his three books of poems are the award-winning *Copperhead Cane* and the more recent *Dialogue with a Dead Man*.

VASSAR MILLER, a well-known and widely published poet from Houston, Texas, has published four volumes of poetry. The most recent is *If I Could Sleep Deeply Enough*, from Liveright, 1974.

ROBERT MORGAN, from Zirconia, North Carolina, is now teaching at Cornell University. His two collections are *Zirconia Poems* and *Red Owl*, published by Norton.

HARRY MORRIS teaches at Florida State University. His collection of poetry entitled *Snake Hunter* was published by the University of Georgia Press.

NORMAN C. MOSER, a North Carolina native who has been living in Texas, is the editor of *Illuminations* and the author of a collection of poetry entitled *Open Season*, to be published by Desert Review Press.

PAUL BAKER NEWMAN teaches at Queens College in Charlotte, North Carolina, and has published widely in literary journals. His third book of poetry is *The Ladder of Love*.

PRESTON NEWMAN teaches at VPI. His poetry has appeared in the *New Yorker, Nation, Poetry, New Republic*, and other magazines.

JOHN NIXON, JR., a native of Mississippi, is co-editor of *Lyric* at Bremo Bluff, Virginia. Winner of the Bellamann Award, he has contributed to *Saturday Review, New Yorker, Mademoiselle, New Republic, Georgia Review*, and other magazines.

LINDA PASTAN, of Maryland, has contributed poems to *Harper's*, *Sewanee Review*, and *American Scholar*. She has published a collection of her poems called *A Perfect Circle of Sun*.

LOUIS PHILLIPS is a native Floridian now teaching at the Maritime College, State University of New York. He has published numerous plays, chapbooks, and a novel entitled *Jonathan Theodore Wainwright Is Going to Bomb the Pentagon*.

ALLEN PLANZ is a Southerner now living in New York. He was poetry editor of *Nation*, 1969-72, and is the author of five books of poems, including *Poor White and Other Poems* and *A Night for Renting*.

STANLEY PLUMLY is a native Virginian now teaching at Ohio University, where he is poetry editor of the *Ohio Review*. His two collections are *In the Outer Dark* and *Giraffe*.

SAM RAGAN, a North Carolina poet, is the owner-editor of the *Southern Pines Pilot* and the author of *The Tree in the Far Pasture* and *To the Water's Edge*.

PAUL RAMSEY, poet-in-residence at the University of Tennessee, Chattanooga, is the author of five collections, including *In an Ordinary Place* and *A Window for New York*.

JULIA RANDALL, who has retired from teaching at Hollins College in Virginia, is the author of *The Puritan Carpenter*, published by The University of North Carolina Press and *Adam's Dream*, published by Knopf.

CAMPBELL REEVES is a native of New Zealand now living in North Carolina. She has published two books of poetry, *Bane of Jewels* and *Coming Out Even*.

ALFRED REID, a former editor of *South Carolina Review* and now a professor of English at Furman, has published two collections of poetry, *Crumbling Stones* and *Lady Godiva's Lover*.

GIBBONS RUARK, a graduate of The University of North Carolina at Chapel Hill, is now teaching at the University of Delaware. His *A Program for Survival* was published by the University Press of Virginia in 1971.

LARRY RUBIN, who teaches at Georgia Tech, has published two volumes of poetry, *The World's Old Way* and *Lanced in*

Light, and has won the Sidney Lanier Prize. A third volume, *All My Mirrors Lie*, will be published by Godine in 1975.

GEORGE SCARBROUGH has been a high school teacher and journalist and now lives in Oak Ridge, Tennessee. He is the author of three books of poems published by Dutton, including *Summer So-Called*.

JAMES SEAY teaches at The University of North Carolina at Chapel Hill and is the author of two collections of poetry, *Let Not Your Hart* and *Water Tables*, from Wesleyan University Press.

JOSEPH EDGAR SIMMONS, a native Southerner, has taught in Virginia and Texas. A winner of the Bellamann Award, he is the author of *Pocahontas and Other Poems* and *Driving to Biloxi*.

DAVE SMITH, a native of Virginia, now teaches at Western Michigan University and is the author of *Bull Island*, *Mean Rufus Throw Down*, and *The Fisherman's Whore*.

FRANK STEELE, who teaches at Western Kentucky University, is a widely published poet and the editor of *Poetry Southeast: 1950-1970*.

LEON STOKESBURY, a native of Texas, is presently teaching at Lamar University in Beaumont, Texas. His poems have appeared in the *New Yorker*, Borestone *Best Poems of 1972*, *New Voices in American Poetry*, and *Intro*.

JOHN STONE teaches at Emory University School of Medicine and Grady Memorial Hospital in Atlanta. His first collection of poems is *The Smell of Matches*, Rutgers University Press.

ROBERT JOE STOUT, a native of Texas, is a journalist now living in California. His latest novel is *Miss Sally*, published by Bobbs-Merrill; his two chapbooks are *Moving Out* and *Trained Bears on Hoops*.

DABNEY STUART, who lives in Lexington, Virginia, has published three volumes of poetry, *The Diving Bell*, *A Particular Place*, and *The Other Hand*. He is poetry editor of *Shenandoah* and an associate professor of English at Washington and Lee Univeristy.

HOLLIS SUMMERS, poet, novelist, and short-story writer, is a native Kentuckian now teaching at Ohio University. Recent books of his poems include *The Peddler and Other Domestic Matters, Sit Opposite Each Other,* and *Start from Home.* His latest novel is *The Garden;* a recent collection of short stories is *How They Chose the Dead.*

ELEANOR ROSS TAYLOR has published two collections of poetry, *Welcome Eumenides* and *A Wilderness of Ladies.* She and her husband Peter Taylor live in Virginia.

HENRY TAYLOR teaches creative writing at American University. His *The Horse Show at Midnight* was published by Louisiana State University Press.

WILLIAM E. TAYLOR, formerly editor of *South,* is head of the English Department at Stetson University. He is the author of four collections of poetry, including *Down Here with Aphrodite.*

ROBERT WATSON teaches at The University of North Carolina at Greensboro. He has published a novel and four collections of poetry, the latest being *Selected Poems.*

GAIL BROCKETT WHITE, a graduate of Stetson University, edits *Caryatid* and has published a book of poems, *Masque.*

JAMES WHITEHEAD teaches creative writing at the University of Arkansas. He is the author of a collection of poetry, *Domains,* and a novel, *Joiner.*

MILLER WILLIAMS is presently teaching at the University of Arkansas. He edited the recent collection *Contemporary Poetry in America.* Among his own books are *So Long at the Fair* and *The Only World There Is.*

EMILY HERRING WILSON, active in the Poetry-in-the-Schools Program in North Carolina, is the author of *Down Zion's Alley.*

CHARLES WRIGHT was born in Tennessee, went to college in North Carolina, and now teaches at the University of California at Irvine. His second full-length collection, *Hard Freight,* was recently published by Wesleyan University Press.

CHARLES DAVID WRIGHT has taught in the creative writing program at The University of North Carolina at Chapel Hill. His first collection, *Early Rising,* was published by The University of North Carolina Press.